ACTING From The INTELLECT

An acting method for actors who use their mind

O

Originate Press

From Award-Winning Actor & Filmmaker
NATHAN CLARKSON

Acting From The Intellect:
An acting method for actors who use their mind
By Originate Press
Copyright 2024 Nathan Clarkson

ISBN 979-8-9872819-2-5

All rights reserved. No part of this book may be reproduced or transmitted in any form or by any means whatsoever without express written permission from the author, except in the case of brief quotations embodied in critical articles and reviews. Please refer all pertinent questions to the publisher.

The Method of the Mind

When I was a new actor, I had grand dreams of mastering the craft of acting. I had visions of myself in films and on stages, where I would give award-worthy performances to an awestruck audience who would count my name and work worthy to stand in acting history alongside the greats. But I didn't just want it — I did something about it. While I was still a teenager, I left my small town with big dreams and headed to New York City to attend acting school. It was there where I studied under some of the greatest acting instructors in the world, who taught me the words, ways, and methods of Meisner, Hagen, Stanislavski, and more. It was there, in the day in, day out study and practice of these invaluable but incomplete methods that I began seeing the through line that tied each of the acting philosophies together — the commonalities that existed in each of them, even through their apparent differences and approaches.

As far as I could tell, even though each of these methods were unique, they all contained a common core and emphasized a common goal: to put the actor in touch with their emotions. This comes from the belief that humans are primarily emotional beings, so to give an authentic performance, the actor must be in the emotional state of the character they are playing. This emotional state is achieved through a variable of methods including but not limited to:

- "Sense Memory" (recalling through your senses your personal memories to inform your performance)

- "Method Acting" (the practice of fully living out, even when not acting, the character and their physical, mental, and verbal realities to make the actor feel as though they *are* the character)

- "Emotional Preparation" (taking time before the scene through the use of music, memory, or other means to put oneself in the emotional state of the character they are portraying)

- "Emotional Substitution" (the practice of digging up your own memories, sometimes even traumatic ones, to use and translate those emotions to feel the same thing as the character)

There are many more methods of acting that revolve around the practice of trying to feel something, to connect the actor more strongly to their emotions. And these can be valuable assets in getting into the humanity of a character to give an emotionally authentic performance. But humans are more than just "emotions." We are more than just the sum total of what we feel, so these methods that revolve only around making the actor "feel" something are incomplete and lacking when it comes to helping an actor give their best performance by inhabiting a character holistically.

I remember in one of my first acting classes, after getting frustrated at our class' inability to perform emotion well, our acting instructor started screaming and throwing books, then knocked over a table, then turned to us frightened students and said, "That is acting." From that moment, we all took to heart that "real" acting is simply showing large displays of emotion. And in our scenes over the course of the months following our teacher's emotional display, in effort to be real actors, we began an unspoken competition of who could show the most and biggest emotions. Our scenes suddenly were full of crying, yelling, even physical fighting – all in effort to give the best acting performance because we were taught that real acting is simply big and loud emotions. And while this felt good and seemed right, I noticed my tendency to rush towards emotions in a scene, even when it didn't make sense for the circumstances or character. In our attempt to connect to our emotions and be "real" actors, I noticed that most of our scenes started to look a bit one-note. I noticed that the reality we were supposedly meant to be reflecting accurately was anything but one-note, and wasn't always just a matter of emotion.

Sometimes a scene calls for high emotive displays, but sometimes great acting is small. Sometimes a moving performance is a character trying *not* to cry, or keeping calm in desperate situations, or simply displaying the subtle realization of life-changing information. Great acting isn't just big, showy, emotional displays; great acting is a performance that makes sense. Emotions are part of the human experience, but they are not the total of the human. We are more than what we feel. And practically speaking, relying entirely on our ability to enter an emotional state to achieve a quality performance has many practical negative ramifications.

When I was a young actor, I believed as many (or most) do – that you need only to rely on tapping into your feelings to act well. And while I never "felt" that I was as natural as my classmates at the "feeling" aspect, I gave it the old college try, so as not to disappoint my dream of mastering what I was told was the craft of acting. And while in acting school, this was fine. I was given time to do "emotional prep work," I was given space to find my groove, I was guided along the process every step of the way. But when I left acting school and booked a real role on a real TV show, I suddenly found a very different reality. The producers and director didn't have time for me to "emotionally prepare" before the scene, much less in between thirty takes. They were on a tight schedule and needed to get their shots. There was no time to sit in a corner digging up memories from my past, nor was there space to slip into the "vibe" I was led to believe was so integral to my work, as a million crew members carrying large equipment and extras running to and fro whizzed past me. I was instead expected to show up, hit my marks, say my lines, and immediately drop into the scene in front of me. If I didn't, I ran the risk of being labeled "high maintenance" and losing out on future opportunities.

A film set is hardly the place for meditation exercises or mindfulness practices. It is a place of work, where I was expected to perform no matter how I felt. This culture shock at the stark difference between my experience in acting classes and the one I found on real life sets was jarring. But it was also the thing that eventually led me to discovering a more practical, more holistic, and more realistic method of acting that resulted in my not only being able to work under less than ideal conditions at a moment's notice, but at the very same time, it also empowered me to give the best, most authentic performances I had in my entire journey as an actor.

~

Over many years, numerous film and television roles, a plethora of hours of coaching actors, and endless thoughts, theories, and writings, I formed, piece by piece, the method of acting that I call "Acting From The Intellect." It has helped both myself and my clients find a practical and potent path to powerful performances that are attainable at a moment's notice. Acting from the intellect is exactly what it sounds like. It is a method where the actor grounds their character and scene work in their mind, an underused and sometimes even denigrated tool that allows the actor to more fully control and bring fullness to their work – particularly the work that lays beyond the walls of acting classes, on real sets and stages.

Emotions are an important part of the actor's focus, but they ought to come secondary to the mind. The mind is the most basic part of who we are. It is the base off which the entirety of ourselves is built. The mind holds our memories, personalities, and thoughts; emotions are simply the human reaction to these elements of who we are. Thoughts inform, shape, and even create emotions. So to give an emotionally authentic performance, we must first master our minds, which provide guidance to the emotions we display.

If in our performances we ignore the mind, not informing or educating it, but skipping over it to go straight to emotions, our performances will be ungrounded, unrealistic, and ultimately, inauthentic. How many times have we seen a new actor try to emulate what they have been told is "good acting" by simply showing large emotion – yelling, crying, or laughing out loud – but ultimately failing to give a connective performance because their emotion is untethered from the reality of the scene they are in and the character they are portraying?

Many young actors wrongly believe that it is emotion *only* that creates an impactful and quality performance. But very often, the most emotionally moving moments in a performance aren't the displays of emotion. Rather, they are moments when the character takes in information, which we see reflected in the nuanced expressions that appear across their face, which ultimately build and inform the outpouring of emotion. The emotion is only the climax to the necessary process that begins in the mind.

Watching only the ending of a movie or play would be far less impactful than experiencing it from the beginning. Seeing the progression of the narrative, the unfolding of the story, builds us to the resolution. Likewise, every moment in an actor's performance is a micro-story the actor is telling – one that might end with emotion, but always begins in the mind.

As we think across the most impactful acting moments in film and stage history – the ones that stay with us, the ones that move and touch us, the ones that appear so real it seems like we're not watching acting at all – we see a common thread: a performer who fully understands with their mind the scene they are in, the character they are playing, and how to let that knowledge (that lives in the mind) influence, shape, and guide their emotions.

Imagine, if you will, a scene where a character loses their job. Upon entering their boss' office, we watch their trepidation as the character uses their mind to assess the situation. Then, when the character's boss says the words "You're fired," we watch the character take in the information, their mental muscles processing the full implications of what this means. If the actor has fully educated themselves on the logistic realities of this character (their personality type, their psychology, what they believe about people, the world, purpose, and authority), all the information held in the mind about the character will inform and produce a realistic and natural outpouring of emotion, be it crying, yelling, or maybe even stoically accepting their fate.

Employing this method of both informing yourself mentally about the character's reality before the scene, and intaking mentally the information during the scene before jumping to emotion, will allow the viewer to watch the entire story of the moment unfold. This will produce an infinitely more powerful and authentic performance than if the actor had not begun with the mind (and also relied on it in the scene) and simply burst into tears, not allowing the audience to see the mental journey that justifies the emotional climax to the scene. To give a truly authentic, emotionally realistic performance, we as actors must begin with the mind.

There's a popular philosophy that to achieve an emotionally powerful state for a scene, the actor can skip over the mind and go straight to emotions by way of "transference," where the actor doesn't need to educate their mind on the character and scene, but instead simply must root through their own life, memories, and experience to find a memory that elicits an emotional response they can then use for the scene they are acting in. Aside from the ethical concerns and the negative personal effects that come from the practice of digging up dark, sometimes traumatic, memories to relive for a performance, I think this philosophy is also a nonsensical one that will not produce the best performance results for the actor.

If an actor is playing a character that is experiencing sadness at being fired from a job, and the way they achieve this sadness is by remembering when their first pet died, it will be a mismatched sadness that can't possibly comport to the needs of the scene or the reality of the character. The sadness of losing a pet is an entirely different sadness than the one experienced when losing a job. Recycling old memories to use as parts in the machine that is a new scene is like using a dishwasher part to fix your car – it might (kind of) work, but it will never fit as it's meant to, and this will limit the car's ability and functionality.

I remember sitting in a one-on-one meeting with a premiere acting coach in Hollywood before joining his class. In the meeting, he asked me to detail a few of the worst, most painful and traumatic memories I had. After, in good faith, I shared a few of the most intimate and painful moments in my life, he sat back, nodded and said these would be useful to him in helping me in my scene work. Wanting to fit in with the acting culture, and believing what the books and methods taught, I joined the class. Over the next months I worked on multiple scenes and characters, and out of the classic emotionally-based philosophies, my acting teacher would bring up the sacred memories I had shared with him so as to attach me to emotion to better serve my work. And while I tried as hard as I could to let these memories affect me in a way that would better my performances, what I ultimately found was that they either produced an emotion that wasn't needed from the character I was playing, or, having mentally healed from the memory I was using, it wouldn't have enough of an emotional effect on me to matter in the scene.

I became frustrated at the lack of effectiveness that this emotionally-based philosophy offered. So, unhappy with my results, I decided to take matters into my own hands. Instead of just trying to feel something by utilizing the classic methods, I began to piece together my own personal method. I began to incorporate my extra-acting studies of **psychology**, which gave me insight into the mind and behavior formed from the past of the character I was playing, **philosophy**, which informed the beliefs and values of my character, and **sociology**, which gave me context for the culture, customs, and behavior my character was living in. And in utilizing study and logic to fully form and put together a mental understanding of who I was playing and the world in which I was playing him, I then found the **implementation** of those realities through my natural human empathy. These facts coalesced in my mind in a way that suddenly transformed my performances from disjointed and inconsistent emotional displays, to fully realized, authentically emotive, and humanly true performances. Through my newfound method, I was able to fully inhabit my character's world instead of trying to fit them into mine. This made it possible for me to portray an actual character, not just a caricature.

My acting teacher noticed immediately. He quickly recognized the stark difference in the quality of my acting, praising me and himself while wrongly attributing the growth to his method and being entirely unaware that it was actually the result of *ignoring* his advice (based off of a century of emotionally-based philosophies). The difference was only credited to me choosing to use my mind as the central starting point off of which I built a better acting craft.

The entirety of the human experience is filtered through the mind, which is what I'm going to help you develop and connect to your acting work in the coming pages.

If you join me on this quest, I will be taking us beyond the walls of "acting" culture into the sea of the wide and real world that we seek to portray in the projects we are a part of. And I know this is a departure from most of the sentiments found in today's actors and acting teachers. There's an unsaid philosophy that's created a culture of actors who believe studying anything outside the "acting world," reading acting books, and exploring acting methods is unneeded, or even a waste of time when going about improving our craft. But stepping beyond the world of "acting" just might be the most helpful thing we can do in becoming better actors. Stepping outside the bounds of the "acting" world will give us a greater access to the studies and collective knowledge that give us insight into the human person and the human condition — which will prove itself to be an invaluable practice as, it turns out, the majority of both the characters we portray and the audience who will view our work, are, in fact, human.

I've deciphered four necessary elements of what it means to act from the intellect, three paths we must take to fully employ this method. They are unlike many popular previous methods, but I believe this to be a good thing that might just take you from a caricature to a character. Shall we?

Element 1:

Psychology

Psychology
[psy·chol·o·gy] ***noun***
The science of mind and behavior

For an actor, the Webster's Dictionary definition of psychology should inspire immense interest and study in the subject, for in it lay the keys to unlocking the characters we are called on to play. Simply stated, in plain terms, psychology is the peeling back of the veil, offering us a peek inside the inner workings of a human soul to understand why they are who they are. And while psychology is often overlooked in many methods of acting, we see here in both the official and colloquial definition that psychology gives us insight into how a person thinks and how that will affect how they will behave. This is an invaluable tool to understanding the characters we are given to play and why they act the way they do.

I once was given a role in a TV series where I was to play a struggling addict trying and failing to put his life back together. Seeing the obvious pitfalls of "methoding" the role by "becoming" the character via getting myself hooked on illicit substances, I instead opted to prepare myself for the role by meeting with a revered acting coach in Hollywood. We spent an hour going over the scene, with him using my difficult memories to try and help me tap into the emotions of the character. After the coaching session, I believed myself to be adequately equipped with the necessary tools to act out the part by readying myself with my own experiences in an attempt to bring about an emotional state to perform the role I had been given. But when I got on set and the director yelled "action," something wasn't right — I couldn't seem to give the performance that the role and the scene needed. Firstly, because I was unable to find the emotional resonance from my memories, as I was distracted by the busy set filled with lights, props, and people walking to and fro. I didn't have time to go off and do the "emotional prep work" I always had in class. But even if I did, I couldn't keep it up for ten takes in a row, especially with the director and DP putting me into physically uncomfortable and unnatural positions to get the shot. Then, secondly, the emotions I was able to conjure up from my memories didn't seem to match the ones required for the scene. I was showing emotion, but not ones that had the depth, nor shape, that an actual addict would feel. So the first few takes felt wrong and inauthentic. When I had worked with the acting coach, in the quiet, wide open space of an acting studio and all the time in the world to "get it right," we had rightly ascertained that the character of an addict would be one filled with shame and desperation. But there, on set, as I was performing the scene, I suddenly realized that the shame and desperation I had felt in my personal life wasn't the same type that an actual addict would feel — that my character would feel. So, desperate to figure out how to play this character (and fast), as a last ditch effort, I fell back on my years of having studied psychology. I pulled up in my mind the studies and information I had read on addiction, what it did to the mind, and how it made people behave. I let the practical knowledge from my studies inform my brain and suddenly, it clicked. In that moment, I found a more true and authentic connection with my character by leaning on what I had learned, instead of trying to feel something. As I thought about what I knew, my sympathy kicked in. Suddenly, I was able to give what, to this day, I still consider to be one of my best performances.

No two people will react the exact same way in any given set of circumstances. When faced with a situation where a person discovers their lover has betrayed them, one person might scream, yell, and threaten, while another might become closed off and subdued. Similarly, when one person falls in love, they might be exuberant and effusive, while another might be fearful and reflective. The difference in their reaction to the given situation is a result of their psychology. Simply behaving how we would respond (or how we think we should respond) based on our own experience is an inadequate method for portraying the reality of the character we are given. How someone will react is determined by their personality, experience, memories, trauma, culture, and more. Psychology gives us insight into all of this. Knowing which reaction is appropriate is going to be heavily informed by our understanding of the psychology of the character we're playing. So to give a quality performance, we must first understand the psychology of a character.

Luckily, we live in a time where countless psychological studies into countless contexts and minds have been conducted over many decades and are readily available to us to help us better understand every kind of character we will play. If we are given the role of someone who has led a drastically different life than we have, it is far more beneficial to study the mind of that kind of person, than to believe that our experience could ever fully encapsulate theirs.

So what does this mean about how we approach a character — especially ones who are vastly different from us in both experience and personality? It means that if you are tasked with portraying a character who grew up in extreme poverty, you must go and read about the psychological effects that poverty has on individuals. Conversely, if you are portraying someone who grew up with extreme privilege, you will need to educate yourself on what being spoiled or having high pressure at a young age does to the human brain. If you are portraying an abuse victim, you need to read about different kinds of abuse and how it affects the mind and behavior of victims. If you are portraying a murderer, you must study what things lead people to kill in every sort of situation. So on and so forth.

Many of the characters we will play will be entirely different from us. The way into understanding and ultimately portraying them accurately will come from a decision to not just imagine what *we* would feel like, or pretend to have their experience, but instead from doing the harder work of studying to understand their minds, their psychology. From that flows the reality of who they actually are.

Action Steps

- Identify five psychological realities of your character (upbringing, traumatic/impactful life events, personality traits, etc).

- Research the psychological realities of these factors through online videos, documentaries, published studies, books, and articles.

- If possible, speak to a psychological professional (psychologist, psychiatrist, therapist, etc.) about their experience with patients who have the same or similar factors as your character.

Element 2:
Philosophy

Philosophy

[phil·los·o·phy] ***noun***
the most basic beliefs, concepts, and attitudes of an individual or group

Philosophy is the study of what is true, and this is a worthy goal, indeed. But for the actor, we will study it differently than the great thinkers throughout history have. We are not just trying to discover what is true, but rather, what our character *believes* to be true. When we learn what someone believes to be true, we are given the glasses through which they view both themselves and the world around them.

Philosophy is tied very closely to psychology, but rather than exploring the mind and how it was formed and how it works, philosophy explores the concepts and beliefs that the mind holds, which dictate a person's understanding of themselves and the world around them. Knowing someone's beliefs can give us a deep and clear understanding of why they make the choices they do. Psychology is unique to the individual and arises naturally and interiorly from within. Philosophy can be shared by many and it is (more or less) adopted by an individual at different points in their life.

In the last section, we saw the importance of exploring the unique way a character's mind works, and why it works the way it does. But we must now build upon this knowledge of our character by beginning to understand how a person's beliefs affect their understanding of the world, their morals, desires, and ultimately, how they will act in the world.

There are countless philosophies one can adopt and build as a part of a patchwork throughout their lifetime, and while psychology plays a role in what belief system one will choose, philosophy is the guide to how that makes sense in the world. Psychology and philosophy are symbiotic, each informing each other. If psychology is the car of the mind, philosophy is the road it drives upon. Studies have shown that psychology often affects what philosophy one will choose. But philosophy will often affect how one will think.

One chooses a philosophy for a myriad of reasons: their peer or familial influences, their own study of figures and thinkers, or even as a reactionary measure to a particularly influential life event. But whatever philosophy someone adopts, it is the grid and structure by which they make sense of reality.

So to fully understand and give an authentic and informed personification of our characters, we see that understanding what they believe to be true about reality will have a large effect on the accuracy of our portrayals. Imagine, if you will, you are tasked with playing a character who's about to die. Whether their philosophy is one that believes in an afterlife or not will drastically change how this character faces their mortality. If they do believe in life after death, there might be a greater peace in facing their end. If they do not, it's plausible that the character would experience emotions of fear as they confront their fate. But upon further investigation of your character's beliefs, this course could be changed by the millions of little details of someone's philosophy, which is why studying a person's beliefs intently will hone in on the details that will inform your performance. The above analogy could be flipped if the dying character believes in an afterlife, but is worried they'll go to hell and not heaven, or if the character doesn't believe in an afterlife, but believes ceasing to exist will bring an end to their pain.

Understanding as specifically as possible your character's philosophy will give you a far more nuanced and detailed performance. You will be educated with the small pieces of information that make up the machine that is that character's worldview, and how it will affect how the character interacts with the scenes and circumstances of their story.

I once played a sad clown in a feature film who shares with a stranger his plans to end his life. Throughout the film, we discover why the clown wants to stop living and how his philosophy informs that decision. The clown desires to believe that things matter, that he matters, that making people smile for a living matters. But ultimately, because he has adopted the philosophy of nihilism ("the rejection of all religious and moral principles, in the belief that life is meaningless," according to Oxford Languages), he is unable to see any reason or purpose for his existence. To play this character well, I first had to understand his psychology — why he thinks and acts the way he does. As a result, I then understood why he adopted this particular philosophy, a belief about reality. This, in turn, had an effect on his mind, which ultimately informed me as to why he ended up in the place he did and why he was making the choices the script detailed. All of this study created a fully defined mental and philosophical understanding of the character, which enabled me to portray him accurately and effectively.

To understand a person fully, we must build off of what we know of their mental state and investigate their belief systems (what some call their "worldview") — what they believe about the world and themselves. Only then can we create a compelling and true character for our performances.

Action Steps

- Read a book that covers the most popular and widespread philosophies throughout history and humanity. See their similarities, identify yours, practice identifying others, and identify your character's philosophy.

- Ask your friends and family around you what they believe to be the purpose and point to existence, if there's objective morality or not, what they believe about the afterlife, and how each of these things affect them.

- Watch interviews with celebrities, politicians, and influencers. See if you can identify in their words what their beliefs about the world and themselves are. Take note of the correlation of how that seems to affect how they act in the world.

Element 3:

Sociology

Sociology

[so·ci·ol·o·gy] ***noun***

the science of society, social institutions, and social relationships
specifically : the systematic study of the development, structure, interaction, and collective behavior of organized groups of human beings

Sociology is essentially the study of groups of people – how they act, interact, and behave. It's the assessing of cultures, both macro (a country or religion) and micro (a family), and investigating the customs and behaviors of groups of humans, how they act, and why they act the way they do.

Our minds and beliefs are integral and important parts of who we are, but they do not happen in a vacuum. The totality of who we are is shaped strongly by the families and cultures we spend concentrated and consistent time in, especially those we grow up in. When we are born, our brains are particularly open to new information. In the early stages of life, our brains know nothing of how the world works, what is true, what is right, what is wrong, etc. So our minds actively intake all the information around us to understand and make sense of the grand and mysterious world we find ourselves suddenly a part of. Scientists call the time period between birth and eight years old "the formative years." This aptly named phase describes exactly what is happening – we (our minds, emotions, and beliefs) are being formed. How we are formed by the type of family and culture we grow up in can vary greatly depending on the experiences, messages, and customs (both familial and cultural) we experience, which ultimately inform us what the truth about the world and ourselves is.

When it comes to the intellectual actor who's attempting to understand the mind and worldview of the character they are playing, ignoring this element of sociology would be a great mistake. Understanding the culture and social environment in which a character has been steeped and formed is invaluable when trying to understand mentally how they work and who they are.

I grew up living in many different parts of the country and traveling across the world. While there was a basic humanity that existed in every community and culture I found myself in, the cultures, practices, and values of each people varied greatly. The people living on the West Coast had entirely different ways of interacting and socializing than those on the East Coast. The people of the South had entirely different traditions, pastimes, and work lives than those of the North. They each saw the world differently, with a unique lens that had been crafted over many generations, which affected their loves, fears, hopes, values, and morality. And all of those completely unique cultures were still just in one country. I am an

American, but I can see the lingering influences in my own life that my ancestors from the United Kingdom passed down to me, from generation to generation, which has had its own unique affect on me as it mixes with the specific culture I grew up in here in the United States.

But even more specifically, while countries, states, and even areas can have their own societal makeup, looking even closer, we see that every family has their own unique culture in how they celebrate, communicate, discipline, work, believe, and more. There are endless studies that show where you grew up, how much money your family had, who was present in your life, and the traditions and customs you practiced all very deeply affect the person you are and the individual you will become – the kind of temperment you'll have, who you'll fall in love with, who you'll vote for, how you view and spend wealth, and how you'll feel about yourself and others. This certainly doesn't mean you can fully understand someone simply by studying a culture – no one can be diluted to a few factors. But studying an individual's family and culture of origin will prove itself to be immensely informative into the makeup of your character.

There is a consistency of a human experience that ties all of us together. All people have a baseline of humanity that we see in our desires and needs. Every person, no matter their culture, is created to desire love, to long for purpose, to feel pain, and to long for a better world – this is why we start with psychology and philosophy. But how each culture (both micro and macro) goes about practicing and expressing their humanity, based on an endless number of factors, is entirely unique.

To truly understand your character, you must acquaint yourself with the culture(s) that shaped not only the way they see and understand the world, but how they interact and live in it.

Imagine you are playing a character that grew up in a tight-knit rural community where money was scarce. This character will most likely have been shaped with a value for family and loyalty to one's own kind, with a healthy dose of skepticism towards outsiders. They will most likely have a strong sense of their own freedom and feel at home in wide open spaces, and be wary of any who threaten that freedom. They might appear hostile in threatening situations, but show a warmth and gentleness when in the confines of familiar faces and family. This is a character I once played in a movie about a drug epidemic ravaging a small town. And it took me doing the work to mentally understand how a person who grew up in the same kind of circumstances as the character I was playing might interact with the world around him to give an accurate and authentic performance.

But now imagine you're tasked with playing a character who grew up in extreme privilege, with distant parents who had high standards and expectations to live up to the success they themselves had achieved or been handed, alongside an added pressure to fit into the social norms that maintained the image of status in a competitive and comparison-based culture. This character will no doubt live with immense pressure on their shoulders to hide the darker and messier parts of themselves while exuding a confident but coiffed demeanor. They will have learned the practice of suppressing their emotions, which will cause them to look down on or even envy those who are able to more freely articulate their humanity. Having not built strong ties with family, and only competitive, surface-level relationships with peers, they will value humans less and accomplishment more, seeing power, at any price, as the way to survive a cruel and harsh world. This is also a character I played in a movie about a group of privileged young people who indulged in and released pressure through violence one night a year.

Both of the above examples of actual characters I have played, while seemingly opposite, are perfect examples of how important it is to understand the sociological realities of the characters we play.

~

To play a character well, we must understand the world from which they come and the culture that formed them. This is why traveling, immersing ourselves in different cultures, and engaging with people different than us in places different than what we know is an invaluable exercise for the actor. We live in a world that is very resistant to trying to "understand," much less acquaint ourselves with cultures and people who differ from us in a myriad of ways. But as actors, we do not have this luxury. We must choose to break from the tribalistic tendencies natural to the human brain and enter and understand the context of the characters we are tasked to play.

We all have been formed and informed by the "societies" — both micro and macro — that we have been a part of. The sociology of a character will inform you of more than just external realities, like dress, manners, or accent, but also the internal values they've been taught — the customs that rule their behavior, and the hopes and fears they've been steeped in and shaped by. You can take this information and, in conjunction with psychology and philosophy, implement it into your understanding of the character, which will ultimately affect your portrayal as you inhabit fully the human you are seeking to live through.

Action Steps

- Travel to the place, or one like the one (time and means depending) that your character comes from. Stay overnight there (longer if you are able) and immerse yourself in the culture/sociology of the place.

- Watch and read unbiased documentaries and books about the culture your character comes from.

- Interview a friend or individual who has an intimate knowledge of the culture of your character. Ask them about the beliefs, customs, behavior, values, fears, hopes, strengths, and weaknesses of the culture.

Implementation

There's a curious phenomenon that has taken place for the entirety of film acting's history. One that many of us may have noticed, that has left movie lovers and movie producers scratching their heads as to why. The phenomenon I speak of is the fact that oftentimes, stand-up comedians make the best dramatic actors. Over and over again, we have watched as society's jesters and clowns, in an attempt to try something new, take on heavy roles in dramatic films and plays, and end up bringing a depth and heart-touching realness to their performances that stand out as some of the most impactful and moving acting in memory. Sometimes even more so than their dramatically and classically trained acting peers. This has both baffled and bothered actors, as many who study the classic acting methods for years are suddenly outshined by an individual with virtually no acting training. But why does this happen? On its face, it seems absurd that an individual who has made a career of telling crass jokes and getting laughs from scatological one-liners could ever give a performance that touches so deeply the human soul. But while some chalk it up to random chance or luck, the staggering consistency at which the phenomenon has taken place for decades, even centuries, now tells us that there might be something deeper to this seemingly inexplicable thing. I have a theory as to why these comedians are able to pull such quality dramatic performances from what seems to be thin air, and it's one that gets to the heart of what we've been talking about throughout these pages and proves the power of the "Acting From The Intellect" method as entirely useful. The comedian's job is to look at humanity, ideas, and society, and find the idiosyncrasies within them so that they can then translate these elements and observations into a "joke." But this practice of gazing into the human mind, studying common beliefs, and understanding why groups of people act the way they do, is the very same method we intellectual actors employ when going about attempting to translate these elements not into a joke, but a compelling dramatic performance. So when it comes to the preparation it takes to understand and internalize a character so as to give a strong acting performance, the comedian has spent their entire career in practice of intellectually understanding and enacting the three steps we've explored in this book, which enables them to offer some of the greatest performances we've seen.

Any individual or performer who dedicates time and focus to understanding the elements we've explored in this book is equipping themselves with the necessary tools that a quality acting performance demands. But the question now is, how do we translate the knowledge we've garnered from our minds into our performances in a way that will produce the meaningful representations of the characters we are tasked with playing? Below I've detailed a handful of directives on how to take the intellectual truths you now have in your mind about your character and put them into your acting performance.

1) **Practice:** With anything, the more you do it, the better you get at it. This is true for learning an instrument or playing a sport, and it is also true for acting. The more you practice and perform, the more second nature it will become. Practice can be in the form of joining a scene study acting class, or doing as many student films and short films as you are able, or joining a local theater group, or even performing monologues and uploading them online – it is the mere act of acting over and over again.

2) **Empathy:** Empathy, unlike sympathy, is not just trying to feel your own emotions *about* an individual. It's the act of actually attempting to feel the emotions *of* the individual.

Practicing empathy, feeling the emotions of the character you're playing, will be very helpful in your portrayal of them — but only when that empathy is first informed by the intellect through the method we've now learned. When we use our mind, filled with the knowledge about our character to inform our emotions that we act out via empathy, we will be able to perform a fully authentic and evocative performance.

3) **Trust:** Because we are so used to "feeling" being the basis from where we act, it can be a scary thing to be educated on a character, but not necessarily "feel" what we're supposed to be portraying. But in addition to the above mentioned tips, simply trusting that having informed your mind, the center of your being, will have an effect on your performance often is all you need. Many times, even when there is an absence of felt emotion, we are still able

to fully offer a quality and authentic performance relying on nothing more than the things we know to be true about the character we are playing and the scene they are in. Never believe the lie that you must "feel" something to be a good actor. Inform your mind, then trust that your mind will guide your acting decisions into something both true and beautiful.

Acting is a worthy and wonderful art that can make telling a powerful, meaningful, and beautiful story a reality. It is my hope that in the words and ideas of this book you have found a better way to go about becoming a better actor, by way of intellectually understanding humanity, so as to offer a more full and depth-filled performance in whatever roles await you.

The Author

Nathan Clarkson is an award-winning actor who's appeared in numerous popular TV shows, hit studio movies, and beloved indie films. He has acted opposite some of the biggest Hollywood stars and Oscar-nominated actors. He began his career at New York Film Academy, where he studied with some of the greatest living acting instructors, before studying improv at the Upright Citizens Brigade in Los Angeles. Nathan has over a decade of experience in the entertainment industry and, in addition to his many acting roles, he is also a successful filmmaker (having written, produced, and directed five feature films that have been distributed by the largest studios in Hollywood), has won numerous film festival awards, and has trended on the largest streaming platforms. Nathan is also a *Publishers Weekly* bestselling author of more than five books, including the critically-acclaimed memoir, *Finding God in Hollywood*. Nathan is a certified life coach specializing in the arts and has been coaching both aspiring and experienced actors, filmmakers, and artists for years, helping countless creatives achieve both career success and betterment of their craft. Nathan lives between Los Angeles and New York City.

www.ingramcontent.com/pod-product-compliance
Lightning Source LLC
Chambersburg PA
CBHW032102040426
42449CB00007B/1158